LEADERSHIP MASTERY FOR TODAY

The Six Essential Skills You Need to Take the Lead

BY

Ron Engeldinger

Get a Free Book

The **Success Guidebook** is available free to readers of this book. It guides you though a step-by-step process that you will use to create the life you are meant to lead.

Easy to understand exercises are designed to lead you through the steps of planning and achieving the life you want.

This is the ideal companion to this book and to the author's other book *Your Plan for Success A step-by-step guide to create the life you are meant to lead*.

Get your free copy of the **Success Guidebook** here:
ronengeldinger.com/special_offer/

Ron Engeldinger
Visit my website at www.DrRonengeldinger.com

Printed in the United States of America

First Printing: January 2019

ISBN 9781793889362

CONTENTS

INTRODUCTION

What is leadership? What makes some people effective leaders while others struggle? Are certain people naturally born with the traits that make them good leaders, or can anyone become a successful leader? While experts may offer differing answers to these questions, I firmly believe that everyone has the capacity to become an effective leader.

The study of leadership is not a perfect science. There is no simple prescription on how to be a successful leader. Even the best leaders can make mistakes, and they can unintentionally lead their teams astray. In spite of that, there is a mindset that we can adopt, and there are behaviors that we can learn, that will enable anyone to become a more effective leader.

Many individuals in today's workforce are finding themselves thrust into a leadership role that they may not feel they are prepared for. Whether it is a small team or a large organizational work unit, whenever a group of people works together to achieve a goal, a leader must step up. This book is designed for anyone who wants to be able to shine in these situations and lead the group to success.

I have held leadership roles throughout my life, and I share the insights in Leadership Mastery that I have gained through my own endeavors and by studying the successful leaders whom I have encountered. I will also share what I have learned from the experiences I gained as I coached the future leaders in the organizations that I worked for. My goal is to impart to you what I have discovered, so that you will understand what makes an effective leader. This book will give you a valuable understanding of leadership that will make you better prepared to meet the challenges you face as you are called upon to take on greater responsibilities.

Leadership is not a passive activity. Think of your team's activity as a bus trip. Someone must start the engine. She or he must steer the proper course. That person must accelerate when it is appropriate and they must apply the brakes when necessary. This is the team leader. Along the way, the team leader will ask for and listen to suggestions from the team members about such topics as the best route and good places to rest. However, a successful leader cannot sit in the back of the bus and go along for the ride. Without the team leader driving the bus, the destination might be reached but the road will likely be bumpy and the path may be convoluted.

The tips that you are about to read have been proven to create long-lasting results, allowing you to move forward in your leadership roles. Each chapter will give you a new understanding of effective leadership, and how you can fine tune the skills that you already possess.

Don't miss out on the opportunities for leadership that await you because you are unsure how to proceed, or because you lack the confidence to take on the responsibility. You can become the type of person who understands what it takes to become an effective leader and demonstrates those leadership skills.

In this guide you will learn the important aspects of leadership and the practical steps you can take to improve your skills. Leadership is a complex process, and no matter how much experience you have in leading others, you will gain a new understanding about the topic that will allow you to hone your skills.

HOW TO USE THIS BOOK

Leadership is a complex process, and a lot of information is presented in the following chapters. As you read, reflect on your own leadership encounters. Think about the good leaders you have worked with, and also consider those leaders who have frustrated you. Take the time to relate the concepts in the book to your own experiences.

To get the most out of the book, have a pad of paper or a notebook handy as you read. Jot down ideas that the book inspires. Note areas you can work on and think about how you can best apply some of the suggestions that are presented.

Use your notes to develop a plan of action. Take small steps – you don't need to implement all of the changes at once. When you find yourself in a leadership situation, refer back to your notes and re-visit the relevant chapters of the book.

CHAPTER 1 – BUILDING THE LEADERSHIP MINDSET

Think about the leaders you admire. Whether it is at work, in government or sports, or in a social organization, you regularly come in contact with or observe from afar, leaders in all aspects of your life. You have probably noticed that some leaders are more successful than others. Some people lead their teams to achieve amazing results, while others struggle to get the team to accomplish anything.

Leadership is a multifaceted topic, and there is no formula that you can follow that will automatically make you become a better leader. Becoming an effective leader takes work. Over the years, academic researchers have developed a variety of theories about what makes someone a great leader. None of these theories provides a complete answer to the question of what makes a good leader.

Throughout the course of my career, I have participated in hundreds of team interactions. At times, I was a team member working under the leadership of someone else and, more often, I was called upon to lead the group. Many of the teams that I was associated with were successful and delivered amazing results, while others failed to achieve their mission. It was always an exhilarating feeling to be a member of or the leader of a team that accomplished its objectives.

The Leadership Mindset

I believe that everyone possesses the ability to be a leader. In this book, I am not going to give you a specific recipe with the exact steps that you must follow to become a leader. Human interaction is too complicated a process for that. What I will provide is a set of tools that will guide you in developing the leadership skills that you already have. You will use these tools to develop the Leadership Mindset.

A Leadership Mindset is a way of thinking about human interactions. It guides the leaders' actions as they discover what makes groups of people flourish when they work toward a goal. It is an understanding about the concepts that fuel leadership excellence. By recognizing the essential traits of skillful leaders, and purposefully working to develop them in yourself, you will continue to develop the skills that will make you an effective leader.

The Six Essential Skills of Effective Leaders

Throughout my career, I have observed leaders who regularly guided high-performing groups. The leaders whom I regarded as the best shared a set of characteristics that made them, and the groups they led, more likely to succeed. Among the many ways of thinking about leadership, the leadership standard that I observed to be most effective is often referred to as transformational leadership.

Transformational leadership is an approach that creates positive change. Transformational leaders create a vision to guide the team. They encourage and motivate their followers to innovate, change, and grow. These leaders motivate their teams to achieve significant results. They serve as role models and create an atmosphere where team members will develop into effective leaders.

Here are the traits and characteristics that are demonstrated by exemplary transformational leaders. In the following chapters we will delve more deeply into each of these characteristics, and you will learn what you can do to strengthen the leadership skills that you already possess.

Communication

Communication is an essential aspect of leadership. Good leaders create and maintain an open process of communication. This is a two-way line of communication that encourages team members to offer input. It is not a strict top-down flow of orders from the leader.

Successful leaders inspire the team members by setting goals that are achievable, and they effectively communicate those goals. At the same time they challenge the team members to perform to the best of their abilities. At times, leaders step out of their comfort zone and encourage others to do the same. They empower the staff to offer suggestions and encourage them to make decisions when appropriate.

Commitment

Strong leaders inspire commitment. It is a commitment to the group's shared objectives rather than allegiance to the leader per se. The type of personality-based blind loyalty that discourages dialogue and expects team members to follow orders without question can lead the team to disastrous results. Trust is a key component of leadership. Team members must feel that they trust the leader and, at the same time, the leader has to have confidence that he or she can trust the members of the team.

A centerpiece of leadership is getting buy-in from the team. Helping the group members understand the "why we are doing this" is an important aspect of telling them what needs to be done. People are more strongly motivated to take an action when they know why taking that action is important. This means that the leader has to share information appropriately. Does that mean the leader has to share everything with the group? No, it doesn't. It means that there must be enough transparency to keep the team headed toward the group's goals.

Collaboration

Good leaders foster collaboration and maintain an open dialogue. Listening to what the team members say is as important as telling them what needs to be done. Listening to the team members concerns, objections, and suggestions will give them an investment into the decisions. Even when they disagree with the ultimate decision, the team members will be more inclined to accept the leader's decision and follow the directions if they feel they had an opportunity to provide input.

Delegation is a key component of strong leadership. Leaders often hesitate to delegate important tasks because they fear the other person will not do the job in the same manner as the leader would have. The world is constantly changing, so skillful leaders are always open to change. Problems will emerge that the leader and the team had not expected, so overcoming these new problems may take a change in mindset, and they may need to look for new ways to approach the issue.

Over the years, I learned that when I delegated responsibilities, my subordinates didn't always do the job in the exact same way I might have. However, I made sure they understood the outcome that was expected, and they knew that I would follow up to ensure that outcome was achieved. I realized that they often came up with better, cheaper, or more effective solutions to the problem than I would have.

Consideration

No one has all the answers all the time, so effective leaders encourage problem solving. In my experience, I found that by describing the problem and then listening as group members join a dialogue around possible solutions often led to a suitable solution that I had not considered. Leaders do not always have all the answers, so encouraging an environment of consideration can lead the team to unanticipated successes.

Pushing the team toward its goals without providing the tools and support that are necessary for the team to achieve those goals makes it more difficult for the team to succeed. Providing resources is an important component of leadership.

Constancy

Leaders who display constancy demonstrate integrity and fairness in everything they do. Strong leaders are dependable and reliable. They follow through on their commitments. At the same time, they establish the expectation that all team members will follow through on their individual responsibilities.

Exceptional leaders are generally self-reflective. They understand that they are human and can make mistakes. When they do make a mistake, they accept responsibility rather than blaming others. Great leaders also understand that their success depends on the actions of the entire team, so they share the credit when the team is successful.

Confidence

Exceptional leaders are confident, yet they are not arrogant. They value the contribution of all their subordinates, while at the same time offering honest and constructive feedback. The leader knows that the goals of the group are attainable, even if they will be very difficult to attain, and sets that expectation for the group.

A leader displays a positive attitude that inspires the team to reach for objectives that might test the limits of the team's capabilities. The leader encourages the team members to look beyond their self-interest and recognize that achieving the team's goals are in everyone's best interest.

In the following chapters, I will describe the important qualities and the expertise that strong leaders display. I will help you evaluate yourself in regard to these skills and traits, and provide suggestions for improvements that will increase your skill and confidence as you take on leadership positions in all areas of your life.

Chapters two through six offer detailed insights into how to master the Six Essential Skills that will make you an effective leader. Chapters seven through eleven provide additional tips on what makes good leaders stand out.

CHAPTER 2 – A LEADER COMMUNICATES

Communication is an essential aspect of leadership. Good leaders create and maintain an open line of communication. This is a two-way line of communication that encourages team members to offer input. It is not a strict top-down flow of orders from the leader.

Successful leaders inspire the team members by setting goals that are achievable, yet at the same time challenge the team to perform to the best of their abilities. At times, leaders step out of their comfort zone and encourage others to do the same. They empower the staff to offer suggestions and encourage them to make decisions when appropriate.

Leaders, by definition, must have followers. It is common sense that interaction with other people is the fundamental element of leadership. Whether it is a small team working on a project, or the division of a large company, whenever a group of people get together to work toward a common goal, someone will assume a leadership role for the group. Often leadership is formalized, as in the organizational structure of a company. In that case, the leaders are officially designated. At other times, a group will form without an established leader, and someone will emerge as the group works together.

The key to the interaction between the leader and the group members is effective communication. Good leaders are good communicators. However, what good leaders communicate, and how they communicate, is often misunderstood. A person who is constantly just giving orders is not necessarily a good communicator.

Good leaders create and maintain an open line of communication. This is a two-way style of communication that encourages team members to offer input. It is not a strict top-down flow of orders from the leader.

The challenge that all leaders face is to ensure that each of the members on the team recognizes what the goals of the team are, and also has a clear understanding of what his or her individual responsibilities are. At the same time, it is incumbent on the leader to foster cooperation. When I look at a teams that are failing to accomplish their goals, I often find that lack of cooperation is at the root of the team's dis-function.

Encourage dialogue instead of discussion

We often use the words discussion and dialogue interchangeably to describe a verbal interaction between two people. There is an important difference, however. A discussion has argumentative connotation. Participants in a discussion are most interested in advocating for their point of view and challenging other points of view. Much like in a debate, people involved in a discussion are mainly interested in convincing the other party to come to agree with them.

In a dialogue, the participants are seeking a shared connection. They listen to the other's arguments, seek to understand those arguments and work to develop a collective point of view. The goal of dialogue is the development of a shared sense of connection.

When possible, the team members should be offered the opportunity to provide input into the team's goals. When they have a chance to provide comments and suggestions, team members are more likely to understand the actions that the team is taking and be aligned with the group's vision.

Communicate the vision and objectives appropriately

As the leader, it is your responsibility to determine the final form of the team's objectives, or to communicate directives that came down from higher management. When you do that, make sure that you circle back with the individual team members who offered input. Show them that you appreciate their input. Explain why you disregarded their suggestions, if that was the case. Your team will never function to its best ability if the team members do not buy in to the team's objectives.

If there is no opportunity for the team members to provide input, such as when the orders are handed down from upper management, then the leader must be able to explain and, if necessary, defend the decision to the team members. As the team leader, you must present the goals and action plans to the group and ensure they are clear about what is required of them. Even in this situation, leaders can use dialogue to understand how team members are responding to the orders they have been given and allow their thoughts to be heard.

In my career, the most difficult situations for me were when I personally disagreed with the directives that I was given. When this occurred, I talked to my supervisors to try to understand their reasons for the decision. Even if I disagreed with my supervisor, my position required me to lead the team to successful results. Armed with information about why the particular course of action was chosen, I was able to defend the decision and display a positive attitude to my subordinates.

While teams are working on a shared goal, the members of the team will not always have the same grasp of the end that they are working towards. Is trimming costs the main goal, or is it increasing sales? Team members may also have different ideas about how to accomplish the goal. Leaders who are effective at encouraging dialogue will be able to create alignment while valuing every team member's opinion.

Provide regular feedback

Regularly remind team members about the group's purpose and objectives. When possible, charting the progress toward the team's goals will serve to reinforce the final destination while, at the same time keep team members appraised of the team's progress. A visual representation, such as a scoreboard can make a significant impact.

For ongoing teams, such as a work unit, the objectives might be less easy to represent visually, but it is still important to quantify them as much as possible. Feedback to the group as a whole can be used to motivate, encourage, and also to determine a course correction, if one is needed. In addition, private individual feedback sessions with each of the team members reinforces the dialogue.

For me, regular check-in conversations with each team member was an invaluable part of the communication process. These were outside of the normal performance review process. At times there would be a particular topic to our dialogue while, at other times, it would begin with a general "how are things going?" question that would open the conversation. Rather than summoning the other person to my office, I regularly went to his or her work space (if you are talking about sensitive matters, you should make sure there is a private space for the conversation).

Be an active listener

Listening is an important aspect of communication. Effective leaders pay attention to the person speaking. Paying attention means that you make eye contact and avoid possible distractions. The other person must recognize that you are genuinely interested in what she or he has to say. Good leaders practice the art of active listening.

Active listening requires the listener to focus on the conversation and respond appropriately to what the other person is saying.

You have probably been in conversations where it is clear to you that the other person is not really listening to what you are saying. Active listening avoids this situation. Active listeners display non-verbal and verbal cues that reinforce to the speaker that they are focusing on what the speaker says.

Non-verbal signs include maintaining eye contact, displaying an attentive posture (such as slightly leaning forward), and responding with appropriate facial expressions (i.e. smiling during a light moment or showing sympathy when the situation calls for it). Active listeners refrain from distractions such as looking at the clock, fidgeting, or doodling. These distracting non-verbal cues indicate indifference and a lack of respect.

The verbal aspects of active listening include participation in the conversation. Asking relevant questions that demonstrate to the speaker that you are listening. Questions can serve to clarify what the speaker said and help ensure that you are understanding what the speaker is expressing. Paraphrasing or repeating what the speaker has just said demonstrates your attentiveness, and it moves the conversation into the realm of dialogue. Finally, summarizing what you have just heard so the speaker can correct any inaccuracies will ensure a productive communication.

Use precise communication

Speak clearly and confidently. Get to the point. Provide background information if necessary but carefully consider how much is necessary. A well-thought-out, concise message will communicate your message mush more effectively than a long, rambling speech. Avoid jargon and acronyms unless you are sure the listeners understand the terms.

Check to make sure message is understood. Ask the listener to paraphrase or summarize what you said. This will let you know if the message was received as you had intended.

Key Reminders
- Support open dialogue.
- Convey the vision and goals to the team.
- Be an active listener.
- Offer object feedback.
- Use precise and concise language.
- Utilize check-in conversations.

CHAPTER 3 – A LEADER FOSTERS COMMITMENT AND COLLABORATION

Strong leaders inspire commitment. It is a commitment to the group's objectives rather than allegiance to the leader per se. The type of personality-based blind loyalty that discourages dialogue and expects others to follow orders without question can lead the team to disastrous results. Trust is a key component of leadership. Team members must feel that they trust the leader and, at the same time, the leader has to have confidence that he or she can trust the members of the team.

A centerpiece of leadership is gaining buy-in from the team. Helping the group members understand the "why we are doing this" is an important aspect of telling them what needs to be done. People are more strongly motivated to take an action when they know why taking that action is important. This means that the leader has to share information appropriately. Does that mean the leader has to share everything with the group? No, it doesn't. It means that there must be enough transparency to keep the team headed toward the group's goals.

Teams function most effectively when the leader and the team members demonstrate commitment to the goals and objectives that the team is pursuing. Without a high degree of commitment, team members will end up challenging and resisting rather than taking positive action. However, commitment is a two-way street.

Commitment promotes trust and cooperation, and it is an indicator that the team or organization is functioning at maximum effectiveness. Commitment must grow naturally, a leader cannot force team members to become committed. An effective leader creates the environment that is conducive to a naturally-growing commitment on the part of the team.

Compliance versus commitment

In most organizations, and on most teams, the leader normally is accorded respect by virtue of his or her position as leader. It is generally expected that members will do what the leader tells them to do. However, organizations will not perform at their best when the group members are merely complying with the leader's directives rather than being fully committed to the team's goals.

If they are not fully committed to the team's goals, team members will only do the minimum required of them. For the team to function at the highest level, the team members often need to do more than the bare minimum.

I once led a work group that was assigned to develop a departmental reorganization plan. I assigned tasks to each of the team members, and they carried out those tasks. However, when I reviewed the team's recommendations with upper management, the managers pointed out flaws in the plan. Everyone on the team had done what they were assigned to do, but our plan was not successful. I went back to the team and explained the flaws, and several team members said they were not surprised by management's reaction because they had the same doubts. I asked why they did not bring up their doubts before and the general response was that, "It was not what I was assigned to do."

It was then that I realized the difference between a fully-committed team and one in which the team members were only going through the motions. The people on my team complied with my directives, but they were not committed to the success of the mission.

As a leader, you must accept responsibility for promoting commitment. You cannot assume that the group members will automatically be committed because they belong to the team or organization that you lead. Groups work most effectively when the members trust the leader's decisions and when they feel they are listened to. If team members are going to devote their time and energy to work toward the success of the group, they need to feel that the effort is worth it.

Encourage commitment through recognition and respect

Good leaders have learned the value of acknowledging and rewarding team members for their contributions. For example, work group members need to feel that the organization respects what they have accomplished, so the leader should relate the team's contributions to the goals of the larger organization.

Every team is composed of a diverse group of individuals. Each person on a team brings a distinctive set of skills and talents. They each bring a unique set of knowledge and experiences to the team. To be an effective leader, it is essential that one recognizes the value of this diversity in carrying out the team's mission.

I learned early in my career that I did not have all the answers. Even when I was responsible for leading a team, I found that by respecting team members, and listening to their suggestions and concerns, we could often find a better way to succeed. I also realized that by capitalizing on the skills of each of the team members, we could divide the workload in a sensible manner so that no one person felt overwhelmed.

Inspire commitment through integrity

Integrity is a key feature of a strong leader. Don't make promises that you cannot keep. The leaders that I respected most throughout my career were those who were honest with me, and who I could rely on to do what they said they would do. If, as a leader, you have a hidden agenda or ulterior motive, the people who work for you will not be fooled. You have to be honest with them or they will not trust you, and their commitment will dissolve.

The effective leaders are prepared to answer questions openly and honestly. That doesn't mean they have to share all their information with the group. Many times in my career, I was aware of confidential information that I could not share. When that was the case, I would share as much information as I could and explain that there was some information I was not allowed to share.

Successful leaders also admit when they don't know an answer to a question. When I have been in that situation, I made it a priority to find out the answer and get back to the person who asked the question. Leaders are not infallible, and when they try to act as if they are, it will destroy trust and commitment.

Promote commitment through engagement

As a member of countless teams and workgroups in my work life and also in volunteer organizations, I came to the realization that I felt most motivated when I was fully involved in the group's mission. To know what we were working toward and to understand how my role contributed to the team was exhilarating. When I was a team leader, I could feel a positive energy when the group was fully engaged in the mission and we were all working together. I realized that engaged team members know their roles and responsibilities, and are dedicated to the team's goals. They are focused on the success of the team rather than their individual glory.

Team members are committed when they understand what ends the team is working toward and how they fit into the process. As a leader, it is important that you share your goals and objectives. Clearly spell out what success for the group will be. If your group is part of a larger organization, you should explain how your group contributes to the overall goals of the organization.

Regard team members as partners

Leadership means trusting team members to make the right decisions and respect them as responsible adults, capable of thinking for themselves, encourage them to use their knowledge, skills and experience. Make sure they feel valued. Listen to their ideas and don't reject those ideas out of hand – work to grow them into effective plans.

In all the teams and workgroups that I have been a part of, it was always clear to me that everyone on the team has something valuable to offer. Leaders not only influence followers but they are influenced by them as well

Often team members will make suggestions or observations that the leader had not considered. When the leader listens to what the team members have to say, new solutions to problems arise that are more effective that the original plan. In these cases, the team members feel the leader has respected their opinions. When team members are engaged in the group information processing as partners, they are more invested in the success of the group

Leaders who regard team members as partners rather than followers have a better opportunity to encourage buy-in for new ideas. When they feel they have been listened to, team members are more likely to accept decisions and instructions, even when they do not fully agree with the decision. An effective leader will endeavor to understand the team members' expectations and then make sure the leader's expectations of the group are clearly spelled out.

Key Reminders
- Commitment goes both ways.
- Clearly spell out the group's goals and objectives.
- Explain how the team's goals relate to the goals of the larger organization.
- Make sure everyone clearly knows his or her individual roles and responsibilities.
- Acknowledge team members' contributions.
- Trust the group members.
- Open and honest communication is crucial.
- Involve people appropriately.
- Encourage open dialogue.
- Be visible and available.

CHAPTER 4 – A LEADER SHOWS CONSIDERATION

No one has all the answers all the time, so effective leaders encourage problem solving. In my experience, I found that by describing the problem and then listening as group members join a dialogue around possible solutions often led to a suitable solution that I had not considered. Leaders do not always have all the answers, so encouraging an environment of consideration can lead the team to unanticipated successes.

Pushing the team toward its goals without providing the tools and support that are necessary for the team to achieve those goals makes it more difficult for the team to succeed. Providing resources is an important component of leadership.

In my experience, one of the most important factors in effective leadership is furnishing support for the team members. When the team is lacking the tools required for its success, no leader, even the most charismatic one, can make the team perform successfully. That's not to say that the team members should have carte blanche and have every request fulfilled. It means that the job of the leader is to determine what resources that team needs and see that the team has them. I always felt that this was one of my most important priorities as a leader.

One of the main lessons I learned from my experiences as the member of a team that failed was that leaders cannot make teams succeed by sabotaging the group members. I was a member of the executive team for a large organization when I watched this happen to a colleague. As the director of marketing, he was responsible for developing a pipeline of new customers. However, the president of the organization, the leader of our team, continually undermined him.

From cutting advertising budgets to staff reductions, the director of marketing was continually being asked to do more with fewer resources, and sales slumped. The president regularly berated the director of marketing, blaming the director's lack of effort. When a new president came in, he took a different attitude. He figured out a way to provide the resources that were lacking. He offered support and encouragement instead of criticism, and the sales dramatically recovered.

See to it they have the tools they need to succeed

Strong leaders are sensitive to the needs of the team members. If the team fails to complete its task or fulfill its mission, it is often because the group does not have the resources to carry out their plan. The willpower of the leader cannot overcome the lack of information or tools that the group requires.

As the leader, you are ultimately responsible for the success or failure of the group's endeavor. An important aspect of leadership is determining what the group needs to help it succeed. Open communication is a key here. Talk with the team members individually and as a group to find out what they believe they need. Ask "why" in addition to "what" as you talk with them. Team members should be able to clearly explain why they are making the request and, in the end, it is up to you as the leader to determine how valid the need is.

One of the hard decisions that a leader has to make is how to balance the needs of the group with the resources that you have available. There is never an endless supply of money, time or equipment available, so it is up to you to determine what support realistically can be provided. As the leader, you should always reconnect with the team members to make sure they understand why you made the decisions that you made. One of the quickest ways for a leader to lose the support of the group is to appear to be making decisions autocratically.

Ask them what they need

An excellent way to demonstrate consideration is to ask team members what they need. What additional information or resources will make the job easier? When team members respond with their needs is when a constructive dialogue can ensue. Ask the team members why they feel they need those particular resources. Ask them what alternative resources may be acceptable. Even outlandish requests should be taken seriously and not simply dismissed out of hand. Listening to the team members is the best way I know of to gain their respect and cooperation.

Unfortunately, you will not always be able to provide what a team member asks for. The requested resources could be too costly or, you may come to the decision that they are a luxury rather than a necessity. You might not have access to the requested information, or you may not be able to share that information with them.

If you are convinced that what they are requesting is crucial, then it is time to go to higher authorities in the organization and push for what you need. Prepare to stand up for the group when necessary. The best leaders I have worked under were the individuals who I felt were willing to go to bat for the group. At times that meant standing up to their superiors whether by advocating for resources or shielding the group from unwarranted criticism.

If, on the other hand, you cannot provide what they ask for, you must tell them. That's when the dialogue you have established with the team members is valuable. You will be able to explain which of their requests are possible and what are not. You will be able to work with them to make sure the team does the best with the resources they have.

Be honest with team members

In almost every leadership situation throughout my career, I was in the position of having to say no to requests. I learned that when I failed to clearly explain why I said no, it led to resentment and loss of respect on the part of the team members. When I was able to explain the situation, I found that they showed a better understanding and acceptance of my future decisions.

The worst leaders I encountered in my life were the ones who were not open and honest with the team members. They were the leaders who no one wanted to work with. Leaders such as that can be successful for a short time but it is not a sustainable way to operate. Eventually team members will realize that they are not being treated with the respect they deserve, and the team's results will suffer. High performing teams require everyone on the team to be working together toward the same goal.

Encourage problem-solving

As a leader, you must always be aware that challenges will arise. The times when setbacks occur, such as resources in short supply or obstacles to overcome, are the times that the leader has to step up. I was always able to recognize a strong leader by watching him or her when things weren't going smoothly.

As the group leader, you should always be prepared to lead the problem-solving process. When problems arise, you and the group will have to develop new ways to attack the issue. I have led hundreds of problem-solving sessions, and I learned early in my career that the key to effective problem-solving is to begin with an open mind.

Consideration means recognizing that you do not have all the answers and realizing that the team members can play a valuable part in the process. Take advantage of the skills that each of the team members brings to the group as you search for new ways to solve the problem. In a later chapter, we will delve into the problem-solving process more deeply.

Brainstorming with the group is an effective way to get the members involved in the process. When the group members have the chance to offer suggestions and provide input, they will generally be more committed to the ultimate course of action. By describing the problem and then listening as group members contribute to the dialogue around possible solutions, the group often develops a suitable solution that you, as leader, may not have considered.

Key reminders

- Allocate resources effectively.
- Ask them what resources or assistance they feel they need.
- Communicate your decisions clearly.
- Undertake problem solving with an open mind.
- Encourage group dialogue.
- Stand up for the group and advocate for necessary resources.
- Recognize the fact that each team member brings a unique skillset.

CHAPTER 5 – A LEADER DEMONSTRATES CONSTANCY

Leaders who display constancy display integrity and fairness in everything they do. Strong leaders are dependable and reliable. They follow through on their commitments. At the same time, they demonstrate the expectation that all team members will follow through on their individual responsibilities.

Exceptional leaders are generally self-reflective. They understand that they are human and can make mistakes. When they do make a mistake, they accept responsibility rather than blaming others. Great leaders also understand that their success depends on the actions of the entire team, so they share the credit when the team is successful.

Strong leaders foster loyalty. However, loyalty goes both ways. I am not talking about the blind loyalty that some poor leaders expect simply by virtue of their position. What I am talking about is a shared loyalty to the objectives of the team. The team members work towards the leader's goals because their goals are aligned with the leader's goals.

Attempting to lead through intimidation and fear might work for a short time, but it is not a strategy that can be sustained. Followers will rebel, they will sabotage, and many of the best will leave. An atmosphere of intimidation breeds disloyalty. Many new leaders mistakenly believe that their job title or position of authority will automatically make the team members respect them. A leader has to earn the respect of the team.

Loyalty arises from respect

Do not expect the team members to enthusiastically follow you simply because of your position in the organization. I learned this in my first job as the manager of a small pizza restaurant. I developed a work schedule for the employees without consulting them. In doing that, I failed to take into account the strengths of each employee. Some employees were very efficient in the kitchen but less comfortable in the customer service areas. Other employees were great with the customers but less adept at food preparation.

The entire operation struggled for a time because I did not consider the employees' strengths and weaknesses when I scheduled. Employees were frustrated, morale was low and both the kitchen efficiency and our customer service lagged. Some valuable employees quit.

I only realized my mistake when, at a staff meeting, I asked the employees what we could change to become more effective. Their answers surprised me – they were frustrated with my leadership because they felt I was not utilizing their talents very well. I listened and changed the scheduling process. With the employees providing input into the schedule, morale and efficiency improved. In a short time, my relationship with the employees was transformed into a relationship of mutual respect.

Follow through on commitments

How do effective leaders demonstrate their constancy? They do it through both their words and their actions. When they commit to doing something, they follow through on that commitment. If your team needs additional resources and you agree to take the issue up with your supervisor, make sure you follow through and actually take it to your supervisor. There were many times in my career that I agreed to take a request to upper management even though I felt certain that the request would be denied.

The important thing was that I followed through on my commitment. These requests were often denied, as I expected they would be, but occasionally they were granted. No matter the outcome, I was able to truthfully go back to the team and provide a report on the results.

I once worked for a manager who regularly failed to follow through on this type of a commitment. When he felt the request was futile, he wouldn't even take it to his supervisor. He simply went back to the team and told them the request had been denied. Eventually, some of the team members figured out that he was not following through, and that he was lying when he said he had. Eventually, the team dissolved into chaos and became dysfunctional. The team's mission was never accomplished and the team was eventually dissolved.

Hold the team members accountable

The other aspect of commitment is to make sure that you follow up on the commitments that team members make to you. Whether they volunteer for a task, or are assigned a particular duty, they must be accountable to you and to the other team members for the completion of the assignment. This begins with ensuring that your expectations are clear. Ask them if they understand what they are committing to do. Don't take a simple "yes" as the answer. Have them repeat it to you in their own words.

It is also an excellent idea to explain to them how you will follow up to ensure they fulfilled the commitment. Will you want regular status reports? Will you be evaluating quantitative data? Without appropriate follow up, you have no way to hold the team members accountable for their contributions to the team. The review process should be an objective evaluation of the performance. By establishing an evaluation process, you are signaling to the team member that this assignment is important, and that you will hold them accountable for completing it.

How you follow up is extremely important, especially when the team member is falling short of the goals that were committed to. You need to delve into why the goals are not being met and are additional resources needed? Is the timeframe unrealistic?

I vividly recall one supervisor I had several years ago who would publicly berate an employee when the employee made a mistake or failed to complete an assignment. He yelled at employees in front of other employees and, at times, even in front of customers. He was not an effective leader – turnover in the organization was very high and employee morale was abysmal. No one respected the supervisor and the team's frustration led to poor job performance and even sabotage. I left the company as soon as I found another job.

By following through on the commitments you make and following up on the commitments that team members make to you, you will build a relationship of trust. As a leader, when you demonstrate that you are reliable, and that you follow through, the team members' loyalty will strengthen. When you show that you are dependable, they will be more dependable in return.

Effective Leaders are self-reflective

Successful leaders know themselves. They know what they are good at doing. They also know what limitations they have. No one is great at everything. Some of us are good at planning, while others excel at the execution of the plan. Some of us are more adept at verbal interaction than others. I learned early in my career that I would have never been a good courtroom attorney. My strength is thoughtful analysis. I can write up a comprehensive argument with ease, however, I am not as adept at making a verbal argument and countering objections. The important thing is that you have to be honest with yourself.

It is also important to learn to assess the strengths and weaknesses of the team members. Start by asking each team member to assess themselves. What do they feel are their strengths? Generally, team members will be anxious to explain what they can do best. I have learned that asking them about their limitations will not be as fruitful. Some of them will be open and share what they fell are shortcomings, however, we are often reluctant to share our limitations publicly.

You will learn much about the team members by listening to them and watching them. Pay attention to their interactions with the rest of the team. Are they better at verbal communication, or are they strong writers? Do they seem more comfortable in a formal meeting or do they excel in a more intimate setting, such as a one-to-one conversation?

Great leaders also understand that their success depends on the actions of the entire team. They share the credit when the team is successful. They accept responsibility for mistakes and they admit it when they are wrong.

Leaders who display constancy display integrity and fairness in everything they do. Strong leaders are dependable and reliable. They follow through on their commitments. At the same time, they demonstrate the expectation that all team members will follow through on their individual responsibilities.

Key Reminders
- Accountability goes both ways.
- Good leaders hold themselves accountable.
- Build trust by being truthful.
- Be aware of your strengths as well as your weaknesses.
- Be dependable and truthful in your interactions.

CHAPTER 6 – A LEADER DEMONSTRATES CONFIDENCE

Exceptional leaders are confident, but never arrogant. They value the contribution of all their subordinates, while at the same time offering honest and constructive feedback. The leader knows that the goals of the group are attainable, even if they might be very difficult to attain, and she or he sets that positive expectation for the group.

A leader displays a positive attitude. This attitude inspires the team to reach for objectives that sometimes will test the limits of the team's capabilities. The leader encourages the team members to look beyond their self-interest and to recognize that achieving the team's goals are in everyone's best interest.

Confidence goes both ways. As the leader, you must demonstrate to the team members that you are confident and capable. If you are constantly second-guessing yourself, or if it obvious that you hesitate making decisions, team members will pick up on that. They will interpret your lack of confidence as indifference, or they could see it as doubt that the team's goals will be achieved.

For the team to function optimally, all members of the group must be convinced that the leader and the other team members are not operating with some ulterior motive. At the same time, the leader must have confidence that the team members are responsible and ethical in their work on the team's assignments.

Operating with confidence

Leaders who display indecision, uncertainty, and hesitation rarely inspire their teams to achievement. Team members have more confidence in, and work harder for, leaders who they perceive to be self-assured. The most dysfunctional teams I have worked on all shared one common theme. They were led by individuals who continually second guessed themselves and who were paralyzed by indecision. These teams struggled because the team members had no confidence in the leader.

The most successful teams that I have been associated with all had leaders who displayed a sense of self-confidence. They had confidence in the team members and they had confidence in themselves. Their self-confidence allowed them to listen to team members' suggestions, to respect the team members as valuable partners, and even to admit when they were wrong. Successful leaders recognize that self-confidence is a valuable trait, and they know it must be continually cultivated in themselves and in their subordinates.

Self-confidence is a state of mind that can be nurtured

We all encounter times in our life when we are not sure what action we should take. It is impossible to accurately predict what will happen in the future and what the consequences of our actions will turn out to be. Doubts may arise in our minds about whether the actions we are about to take will produce the outcome we are anticipating. This uncertainty is often a self-confidence killer.

As a leader, you cannot allow lack of confidence to be the cause of indecision or inaction. While it is natural to be apprehensive about the future, effective leaders find ways to develop greater self-confidence and move forward.

Planning and preparation creates confidence

In my experience, I have learned that the easiest way to bolster my self-confidence is to be prepared. Whether it is a new assignment for the team or a roadblock that we encounter along the way, the more prepared I am, the more confident I am. A strong leader is continually studying the situation and planning actions accordingly.

When it is a new assignment, ask yourself and your team to think about how to accomplish the goal. Are there more than one approach to take to fulfill the assignment? If so, look at the advantages and disadvantages of each one. Think about potential roadblocks and determine possible ways to overcome them. You may not be able to anticipate every possible scenario but, by considering the problems that can arise, you will be armed with potential solutions.

A positive attitude nurtures confidence

For me, a negative attitude and lack of self-confidence feed off one another. When I am feeling positive about my situation and about my life, I naturally feel more confident. I have learned that I can create a greater sense of self-confidence when I start with a positive mental attitude.

Some people seem to have the knack of projecting a positive attitude in even the most taxing situations. What I have found by talking to these eternally positive people is that they are as anxious in certain situations as I would be, but they are able to outwardly project confidence. Without a certain degree of confidence in yourself and your abilities during those challenging situations you become prone to anxiety, panic, and poor decision making.

Take positive actions to improve your mindset

Developing a positive attitude takes work and maintaining a positive attitude in adverse circumstances can be even more difficult, but it is worth the effort. Fortunately, there are purposeful activities you can undertake that will lead to a more optimistic outlook and, in turn it will bolster your self-confidence. Taking a constructive action is the way to reduce the negativity. The actions that you take when you find yourself feeling apprehensive or hesitant will have a strong impact on your demeanor.

It is important to understand that there isn't one particular action that you can take whenever you want to develop a more positive outlook. There are times when one approach has worked for me, but at other times it did not work and I had to try something else. Often many small actions that seem to be inconsequential can add up and be extremely effective. Here is a selection of positive actions I have used to bolster my confidence.

Use affirmations to nurture a positive mindset

Many people use positive affirmations to create a confident mindset. It often works for me. When I am anticipating a situation in which I might be hesitant, I write down the positive thoughts I want to embed in my subconscious. The affirmations are simple phrases that are repeated to yourself over and over. Simple phrases such as "I have the talent to create a successful life" and "Today is a good day to be alive" have been effective for me.

Document your strengths and achievements

Confidence comes from recognizing that you are capable of being successful. You should be purposefully aware of the successes you have had and celebrate them. Most people have the tendency to minimize the achievements they have attained and focus on their past failures. This has always been a struggle for me.

I overcome this tendency by keeping a list of the successes I have had. It is a resume of sorts in that I think about the jobs I have had in the past and write down the times that I was successful. I note my personal accomplishments, no matter how small or seemingly inconsequential. I note the times when I solved a problem, or when I created a new process that worked better than what we had been doing. I also note the times when the team I was leading had successful outcomes. If you give this some careful thought, you will be surprised at how many successes you can list. Whenever, I review this list, I feel a surge of self-confidence.

Take actions to feel good about yourself

I am very self-critical and that often affects my confidence. When I am in a self-critical mood, the only way I have found to break out of it is to take a positive action. By focusing on actions I can take in my diet, exercise, and dress, I become more confident. I attack stressful situations with physical activity.

Whether it is a workout in the gym or simply a short walk, increasing your physical activity will create a more positive mindset. I have also found that I feel better about myself when I dress well. Wearing well-fitting clothes that are appropriate to the situation always works for me.

Gaining confidence through education

Learning increases self-confidence. Effective leaders recognize that the world is continually changing and we must all keep up with the changes. When I graduated from college with a bachelor's degree in a science field and started on my first managerial job, I was pretty naïve about business. I knew a lot about science, but my job was as an assistant manager of a restaurant, so my science background didn't really prepare me for the job. In that position, I was never very confident of my leadership skills.

One of the ways I was able to become more confident was by continuing my education. I took workshops, attended seminars, and studied the topics that I felt needed work. Over time, I became skilled at the business aspects of the job and that increased my confidence as a leader. Throughout my career. I continued to focus on my education. Whether it was formal education in graduate school as I earned an MBA or informal education through seminars and workshops, it was clear to me that continuing to learn was the only way I could build my skillset to become a more successful leader.

Push yourself out of your comfort zone

Whenever I accomplish a new task or tackle a new project, my self-confidence soars. While I have struggled with self-confidence throughout my various careers, I discovered early that my overall confidence increased when I was able to tackle a new project or accomplish a new task. When new assignments arose at work, I volunteered. At first, volunteering for a new assignment seemed daunting but I eventually became comfortable taking on tasks that I had never done before.

One of the best ways to learn new skills and enlarge your comfort zone is to do volunteer work. During my first year as a restaurant manager, I joined a local service organization. I realized that this was a safe space to learn new skills. At the same time, I was making a contribution to the community and that made me feel good. I had never studied business and I was not very familiar with standard accounting practices, so I volunteered to work on a committee that assisted the organization's treasurer.

My work on the committee eventually led to my taking on the responsibility as the group's treasurer. Not only did I learn new skills that helped the organization, I became more confident in my job. The confidence I gained from volunteering with the organization helped me become a better leader at work. I also learned a great deal about accounting that I was able to utilize many times over my career.

Effective leaders display confidence. If you are consistently second-guessing yourself or wavering in your decisions, your team members can become frustrated and demoralized. At the same time, you have to keep in mind that over-confidence can also lead to problems. A confident leader can change her or his mind when presented with new information. A confident leader will listen to the team member's suggestions. Confident leaders make decisions that are supported by careful analysis and admit when new or better ideas arise.

Key Reminders
- Preparation builds confidence.
- Use affirmations.
- Focus on your talents and strengths.
- Feel good about yourself physically.
- Keep on learning.
- Volunteer for new assignments.

CHAPTER 7 – ACCOUNTABILITY IS KEY

Teams thrive on accountability. When the leader and all the members of the team understand that each of them must contribute, and when everyone is effective in carrying out their respective roles, the team will flourish. Sure, there will be roadblocks, setbacks, and problems to solve as the team moves ahead, but when everyone is accountable for the objectives of the team, the joint reliability that successful teams display will keep them moving forward toward their goals.

As the leader, it is your responsibility to set the tone and to craft an environment in which everyone understands and accepts the team's mission, and each individual feels accountable to the team. Accountability can only be achieved in an atmosphere of trust. This trust comes when leaders are holding themselves responsible for the actions of the team and ensuring that all team members acknowledge that their actions jointly will drive the entire team's success.

When the team is functioning in an atmosphere of accountability, team members are allowed to focus on solving the problems that arise rather than pointing fingers. When individuals are focused on placing blame or defending themselves against blame, mutual trust disappears and teams become dysfunctional. Successful leaders understand that accountability can be cultivated, and they endeavor to encourage an environment where it is valued.

The leader must set the example

One of the most important roles that an effective leader undertakes is to cultivate an environment of accountability and to show their commitment to take on this responsibility. When you are the leader, you must set the standard. Show the team that you value accountability by following through on the commitments that you make.

For example, being accountable means being on time for meetings. I have often encountered leaders who called a meeting only to show up several minutes late to the meeting while everyone sat around waiting. Not only is this inconsiderate, it is counterproductive.

The leader of one team I was on was particularly frustrating for the rest of us on the team because he was habitually late to every appointment he made. When he finally did show up, the meetings were rushed and unproductive.

Some people assume that arriving late shows that you are an important person with many responsibilities. In reality, it demonstrates a lack of respect for the others while generating frustration and resentment.

Strong leaders demonstrate their accountability in the actions they take. They reply back to people when they say they will. They complete the assignments that they are responsible for. They are available to team members to answer questions and provide clarification.

Accountability begins with honesty

In my experience, nothing destroys team functioning faster than when the team members think that the leader is not being honest with them. Successful leaders communicate with the team in an open and candid manner. Leaders do not necessarily need to share everything they know with the team but they cannot be dishonest.

As the division leader of a large organization I often found myself in the middle. I was leading a team of managers who were responsible for producing the sales and profit results that top management required. At the same time, I was the member of a team that was headed by the president of the company. As a team member, I was aware of confidential company information that I was not allowed to share with the members of the team I led. When topics arose that I could not discuss, I explained to my team that there was some information that I was not allowed to share. The team respected that explanation because I had cultivated their trust.

Admit mistakes and learn from them

Ineffective leaders think that admitting when they are wrong makes them less successful as leaders. That is not the case. No one is completely infallible. We all make mistakes. Strong leaders acknowledge when they have made a mistake.

Leaders who recognize that asking for help when they need it display to the team that no one person has all the answers. Asking the team members for their suggestions, ideas, or assistance emphasizes to the team the responsibility for the success of the team is shared by everyone.

The key is to learn from our mistakes and make the appropriate adjustments. Continuous course correction is the sign of an effectively functioning team, and the leader must set the example. No one is comfortable admitting they made a mistake, but leaders who are open and honest with the team generate respect and foster cooperation.

Effective leaders take personal responsibility. They are willing to answer for the outcomes, and they do not blame others. They stand up for the team when it is warranted. When teams that I led ran into problems, I always felt that, as team leader, it was imperative for me to take responsibility because the team's performance was intimately related to my performance as the leader of the team.

Approach problems in the team context

When obstacles arise or the team begins to go off course, the effective leader enlists the entire team in overcoming the obstacle. If one of the team members fails to complete his or her assignment, or someone slips up, the response by the leader should be, "What do we need to do to correct the situation?" Publicly blaming or criticizing the individual at fault only leads to resentment and mistrust.

One of the worst leaders I ever worked for was someone who was appointed as president of a small enterprise where I had been part of the management team for more than a decade. The leadership team consisted of six department managers, and we all reported to the president. The weekly management team meetings were excruciating. Almost every meeting consisted of the president telling one or more of the managers what they had done wrong and how poor their performance was.

When I was in his crosshairs, it was an anxiety-laden experience for me. When someone else was being singled out, I felt embarrassed to have to listen to the tirade. All the managers on the team were talented, but the leader created an atmosphere of distrust and everyone was demoralized. The organization's overall performance suffered and that led to more angry tirades by the president. I quit that job less than a year after the president was appointed, and the company that had been very successful for a long time eventually went out of business.

Set clear expectations

One of the primary responsibilities of every leader is to establish and communicate what is expected of the team overall and what is expected of each team member. Roles and responsibilities must be well-defined and thoroughly understood. The leader must ensure that the expectations are reasonable and goals are achievable. Ideally, the leader works with the team to develop the team's goals.

When they have input into the methods and results that are expected, individuals have a stronger ownership and they develop a shared sense of accountability. Many times, however, the ultimate goals of the team are assigned by someone higher up in the organization. In this case, it is important for the team's leader to provide the team with opportunities for input. Maybe the team can be encouraged to weigh in on intermediate goals or specific methods of operation.

In addition to developing a set of clearly-stated expectations, good leaders confirm that the expectations are understood. They make sure that each of the team members can explain the expectations in her or his own words and has opportunities for clarification. Clear and well-understood expectations ensure that the team members are all working in alignment.

Measure the results

Monitoring the progress and reporting the results of the team's endeavors is crucial for establishing accountability. Effective leaders share the results with the team as often as possible. Once again, however, the results are best shared in a way that does not single out one particular individual's performance. I have always found that individual praise for a good job and correction of poor performance are best conducted privately.

Strong leaders ensure that public recognition is most effective when the entire team can be recognized. When the team misses its goals, the leader avoids blaming specific individuals. The attitude of an effective leader is that the group is in it together, and the focus is on developing solutions to the problems and making the necessary adjustments.

Effective leaders promote shared accountability. They see their job as a partnership with the individuals who report to them. They understand that everyone working for them must contribute to a common objective. They seek input from team members and promote an environment where accountability, authority and a sense of ownership exist at all levels of the organization.

Key Reminders

- Hold yourself accountable.
- Be honest with the team.
- Learn from the mistakes.
- Utilize a team problem-solving approach.
- Clarify expectations.
- Measure and report results.

CHAPTER 8 – MOTIVATION THROUGH RECOGNITION AND REWARDS

An important role all leaders must take on is that of a motivator. Motivation refers to having the desire to do something and the willingness to undertake actions towards whatever one wants to accomplish. Effective leaders create an atmosphere in which the team members are motivated to take positive actions.

The question of what motivates employees and how leaders can encourage or facilitate this motivation has become an important issue for leaders of every organization. Highly motivated team members are more likely to exhibit greater creativity, higher concern for quality results, and they are usually more productive than individuals with lesser motivation.

Motivation can some from a variety of sources, and it can be affected by internal factors (intrinsic) or external factors (extrinsic). Intrinsic motivation occurs when individuals are driven by enjoyment, interest, self-expression, pride of accomplishment, or the personal challenge of the work itself. Extrinsic motivation comes when individuals undertake the work in order to obtain some external reward or achieve a certain goal.

Everyone is motivated to some degree by both intrinsic and extrinsic factors. However, some of us are primarily motivated by internal factors, while others respond more strongly to external factors. Strong leaders understand that both types of motivation are important. Leaders cannot force team members to be motivated, however they can take steps that increase the likelihood that team members will be motivated.

Extrinsic motivation occurs when rewards and recognition provide the encouragement for individuals to accomplish the tasks and work toward the team's goals. There are a variety of methods by which leaders can provide extrinsic motivation to the team. Recognition and rewards can make team members feel important and appreciated, and they can encourage desired behaviors. They range from simple to extravagant.

There are two sides to extrinsic motivation, rewards and punishment. While both of these factors can affect the behavior of team members, I always found that the positive approach, rewarding people for good behavior always produced strong and more long-lasting results. The fear of punishment, such as being fired for poor performance may cause employees to comply with the orders given to them, but there will be little commitment to the goals of the organization, and it often leads to marginal performance. When threatened with punishment, people will only do the minimum that is required to avoid punishment. They will rarely become top performers when punishment is the only motivational tool the leader uses.

While intrinsic motivation is more personal, leaders can take steps to understand how each team member is motivated. It is important to create an atmosphere that is supportive of whatever internal motivation drives each person.

Establish an environment to support intrinsic motivation

To some extent, leaders can encourage intrinsic motivation for the team members by providing meaningful tasks and taking care to explain the reasons for those tasks. Clarifying how those tasks relate to the team's ultimate objectives will provide the meaning and context. Clear and open communication is the way leaders can affect intrinsic motivation. A good approach is to privately ask each team member what motivational factors they think are important to them.

Leaders should also take the time to learn what motivates each member of the team. When I look back at the teams I was a member of, a recurring motivator for me has always been the satisfaction I had when I was providing a service to other people. Whether it was offering a positive dining experience to the restaurant patrons or providing a valuable educational experience to my students, my passion for helping others was a very important motivator. I definitely worked harder when I worked for leaders who understood my passion and encouraged me.

Treat team members with respect

It might seem obvious, but treating people with respect is a strong motivational tool for every leader. I know from personal experience practicing common courtesy, listening to what they have to say, and showing appreciation make team members feel that you value their efforts and contributions. In turn, they will respect you. Mutual respect between the leader and the team members generates an atmosphere of positive morale.

In movies, leaders are often portrayed as having no-nonsense drill sergeant demeanor. They bark out orders and the group snaps to attention. This may work at times in a militaristic environment. However, when you look at the lives of the greatest military leaders, you will find that the most successful commanders were the ones who were able to develop an atmosphere of mutual respect. Motivation by fear and intimidation doesn't foster peak performance.

Put positive recognition in writing

Employees want to know that they have done a good job and, even more importantly, they want to know that you notice. Giving credit to the employees who report to you is an important aspect of leadership. Failure to recognize when team members are performing at or beyond expectations can be one of the greatest demotivating actions that teams encounter.

The key to effective recognition is to put it in writing. Most companies use some type of written annual, semi-annual, or quarterly performance review system, but in my experience that system often becomes very formalized and cumbersome.

For feedback to be meaningful, it is best delivered in a timely manner. If you wait for the annual review to note someone's accomplishments, the effect of the feedback can be diminished. A simple, and very effective, method of providing positive feedback is the hand-written thank you note.

I learned the value of thank you notes from an associate manager who reported to me. When someone on our team performed well or had a major accomplishment, she wrote them a short thank you note. This was a strong motivational tool that earned her the respect and deference that indicates effective leadership.

Provide negative feedback appropriately

For me, one of the hardest aspects of leadership is providing negative feedback. While it is a necessary aspect of being a leader, I never have been comfortable doing it. I would rather deliver positive new than point out the negatives. However, when it is done correctly, providing corrective feedback can become a positive motivator.

Everyone makes mistakes at one time or another, and it is important that the leader point out the poor performance so that the team member can make the appropriate corrections. The most important thing to remember is to criticize the action not the person. Team members need to understand that you value them as a person, even when they have done something wrong. Telling someone he is incompetent will only lead to defensiveness, and it will rarely cause a positive behavioral change.

Criticism should always be delivered privately. One of the most frustrating jobs I had was working for a team leader who regularly criticized and yelled at the team members in our staff meetings. It was demoralizing when I was the one being criticized, and it was extremely uncomfortable listening to him berate the others. Turnover in that organization was very high, and we rarely met our growth and profitability goals. The leader would have been much more effective if he delivered corrective feedback in a less public setting.

Celebrate team accomplishments with group rewards

Teams need to know when they are doing well and effective leaders are adept at recognizing the group's accomplishments. When the team reaches a project milestone, commemorate the occasion with a celebratory activity. Food, fun group activities, and time off are examples of ways the leader can tell the group as a whole, "We did a good job."

If you schedule a group activity, take care to engage in activities that are designed so that everyone can participate. The celebration will backfire if you schedule a strenuous physical activity only to find out that some of the team are not physically able to participate. To ensure that the celebration is one that everyone will enjoy, ask the team members for suggestions. The celebration becomes more meaningful when they are able to be part of the planning process.

Make sure the recognition and rewards are appropriate

A particularly effective leader who I worked for made a point of asking each member of the team how they wanted to be recognized. Then he tailored the recognition to each team member's preference. Some people find it embarrassing to be singled out in front of the group, even when it is for praise. For those people, a private conversation or written recognition is more motivational than making a presentation to them in front of others.

Some people value time off while others will prefer opportunities for additional training, assignment to special committees or membership in a professional organization. By asking each member what types of rewards are the most meaningful to them, you will maximize the motivational value of the reward.

When presenting recognition, be clear about what behaviors and actions are being rewarded. Use objective benchmarks and impartial measures as criteria for determining who and when is recognized. It must be clear to everyone what the standards are. As the leader, you want to avoid at all costs the appearance of partiality or favoritism.

Make sure everyone on the team is eligible for recognition. Don't exclude any group. For example, where there are a variety of types of jobs, such the cooks and servers in a restaurant, you have to design a reward system that ensures no group of team members feels left out.

Recognition and rewards can be strong motivators for a team. When the leader creates a positive atmosphere of respect and appreciation, teams can accomplish amazing results. When the team members feel that they are being disrespected and that no one values their hard work and accomplishments, teams struggle.

Key Reminders
- Use recognition and rewards appropriately.
- Provide meaningful tasks.
- Promote mutual respect.
- Put recognition in writing.
- Provide timely feedback.
- Celebrate the milestones.
- Avoid favoritism.

CHAPTER 9 – LEAD BY COACHING

Coaching is an important component of effective leadership. Successful leaders demonstrate the qualities of transformational leadership. That is, they inspire, and they motivate their followers to innovate, change, and grow. Leaders will make their own job easier when they are encouraging the team members to continually improve. Encouraging team members to reinforce the skills they already have and stimulating them to gain increased competences will allow them to take on additional tasks or responsibilities. A well-coached group functions smoothly as a team. This is what leadership is all about.

Coaching can be a group activity, or it can consist of a one-on-one conversation. It depends on the circumstances. Group coaching is effective when the topic of conversation is vital to the entire team. It enables the team members to work together to solve problems and to accomplish goals. Individual one-on-one coaching is appropriate when the issues only effect one of the team's members.

For coaching to be successful, it is essential that the leader builds trust with the followers. Coaching is all about helping the team members improve. It is not about the leader. A well-coached team will perform more effectively and that will reflect positively on the leader, but that increased performance is brought about by the leader focusing on drawing excellent accomplishments from the individual members of the team.

Build rapport

Good coaching requires building rapport and creating a positive relationship. The people being coached must feel comfortable that the coach is genuinely interested in helping them solve a problem, gain a skill, or become more successful at what they are already doing. In a coaching relationship, the coach helps the team members to discover what they already know about the situation and about themselves. Coaching is NOT telling the other person what he or she should do.

Building rapport in a coaching environment is 80 percent listening and 20 percent talking. You accomplish this by guiding the conversation, and you give the team members the opportunity to talk. You should ask open-ended questions. You must learn their strengths and weaknesses. More importantly, you must also learn what they perceive to be their strengths and weaknesses. You should endeavor to find out what interests them, both in the context of the team's goals and responsibilities and in their personal life away from the team. By learning as much as you can about what interests and motivates them, you can tailor your conversations with them.

When I was conducting a coaching session with one of the people who reported to me, I learned through our conversation that she loved gardening. She had expert knowledge about the best plants for particular soil conditions, and she knew what type of care each plant needed. While my knowledge was not as extensive as hers, I knew enough about gardening that I could use our conversations about plants to build a connection. That connection on a personal level allowed us to have more substantive talks as we delved into the work problems she was having. The important takeaway here is that she knew I was genuinely interested in learning about her and the things that fascinated her.

Focus on the other person

A good coach is able to connect with the team members; to help them recognize and acknowledge their strengths. The secret to forming this connection is asking them questions. When you show them that you are genuinely concerned about them, you will begin creating a relationship of trust. Your focus is on how the other person feels about their situation and on helping them to develop a plan.

As you develop a dialog with them, you will probably form your own ideas about what they should do in a particular circumstance. As a coach, however, you want to avoid telling them what you think they should do. Once you tell them what they should do, the conversation then becomes about what you want. You are no longer the coach, you are the boss.

Empower them to search for answers

Your job is not to tell them the answers, it is to help them discover the answers themselves through a dialogue. Frame your conversation with questions that will draw out their thoughts on the topic. These should be open ended questions. "What do you think about...?", "What do you want to accomplish?" or "Why is this important?" are the type of open-ended questions that will help draw out information. Ask them what they think the roadblocks are and how they think we can work to break them down.

As a coach, your goal is to help them clarify their own understanding of the situation and come up with potential actions they can take. For example, when a subordinate comes to me with a problem and asks me what they should do, I begin by asking them what they would suggest that we do. If the action they should take is not immediately obvious to them, I will brainstorm with them by asking them to develop a list of possible actions. Next, we talk about those possible actions. What are the benefits and drawbacks of each (again, we emphasize asking them rather than telling them).

Feedback should be delivered in a nonjudgmental manner

The other aspect of a leader's job that involves coaching is giving feedback to the team members. Constructive feedback is a valuable tool for letting team members know when things are going well, and it is crucial for redirecting performance when things are not going well. Feedback comes in a variety of forms. It is important to provide a balance of positive and corrective feedback. When the leaders' only form of feedback is to criticize the team members team morale will diminish, and performance will actually decrease.

For example, the supervisor of a team I was on was constantly critical of the team members. The only feedback he gave was when a team member did something wrong. He never recognized team members for the things that they accomplished. Team members were afraid to make mistakes but, even when things were going well, the leader found behaviors to criticize. Being on that team was a frustrating experience. Team members did not put forth their best efforts because they knew they would be criticized no matter what they did. The team experienced extremely high turnover as people decided they could not put up with the negative atmosphere.

Positive feedback is the easiest to give. When someone makes an important contributions to the team or achieves a major accomplishment, it is important to recognize that contributor. Be specific when offering feedback, noting the performance and results that are praiseworthy. For example, "You exceeded your sales goal by ten percent this quarter" is much more effective than "You did a good job." The team member has to know what specific behavior you are commenting on.

Offering corrective feedback is often harder for leaders but it is an important aspect of the leader's job. The most important aspect of corrective feedback is limiting the discussion to behavior. The leader must explain the specific, observable behaviors that were improper. The focus should be on describing what occurred without judgement. The leader should avoid disparaging language. Using the terms "good or bad" or "right or wrong" do not give the listener any useful information and can create a defensive reaction.

In both cases, the key to effective feedback is to focus on the behavior and not the person. Explain what the observable behavior is and what the consequences of that behavior are. Leaders must also beware of giving too much feedback. The feedback session should have only two or three important topics. Presenting too many points will only lead to confusion.

Key Reminders

- Coaching is about the other person.
- Ask questions, especially open-ended ones.
- Listen to their answers to your questions.
- Help them discover the answers themselves rather than giving them the answers.
- Performance feedback should be specific.

CHAPTER 10 – LEAD BY INSPIRING OTHERS

Many of the most famous leaders that come to mind are charismatic. They are confident and eloquent public speakers. They inspire others to action. Aspiring leaders often compare themselves to these famous leaders and become discouraged. While not everyone is a naturally charismatic public speaker, anyone can become an effective leader with the right mindset.

You don't have to be an extrovert to be a successful leader. Some of the finest leaders that I have worked with considered themselves introverts. I consider myself an introvert yet I have been the leader of departments that consisted of several hundred employees, and I have led workgroups involving only a handful of people. As I gained leadership experience, I learned that teams of all sizes need leaders, and most of the leadership situations you will find yourself in will be with relatively small groups. No matter what your personality style is, you can be a successful leader.

I also noticed that the worst leaders that I ever worked with were often sociable and talkative. Unfortunately, even though they were outgoing, their primary consideration was themselves. They failed to recognize that the team members were as much or more responsible for the team's success as themselves. Self-centered leaders often fail because they do not value the unique abilities of the members of the team.

Many inspirational leaders are able to outwardly display a quiet confidence even when things are not going well. When the leader is outwardly pessimistic, team members are rarely inspired to give their best effort and rise to the challenge. I have learned that anyone can learn and apply the behaviors that will inspire and motivate groups to perform well.

Display a positive attitude

Exhibiting a positive attitude is a crucial behavior for effective leaders. If you don't show the team members that you believe they can accomplish the team's goals, then the likelihood of team success is low. Even when you have some doubts, you should keep those misgivings to yourself. Your team needs to believe you are confident that the team can be successful.

Have a vision and purpose, and communicate these to the team

For any leader, it is imperative that the people she or he is leading know what they are trying to accomplish. Why has the team been assembled? What is the end goal? What does success for the team mean? Leading a group, by necessity, requires that there is some objective that needs to be achieved. As a leader, you must first clearly understand what that group's objectives are.

Second, you must communicate those objectives to the team and make sure that every team member understands what the goals are. You don't need to be an eloquent or persuasive speaker to communicate the goals and objectives to the team – you simply need to be sincere. Explain this plainly and in your own words, don't try to copy anyone else's style. Be yourself, and your team will see you as authentic.

Be respectful

Respect and common courtesy are incredibly powerful tools to motivate the people you lead. Think about how you expect to be treated by your superiors. That is how you need to treat the members of your team. How do you feel when someone is barking orders at you as if they were a drill sergeant? That approach may be accepted in military training, but it is not an effective way to inspire your team to high performance. You can be demanding without being demeaning by setting the proper tone. You explain to the team that you expect each team member to fulfill their commitments to the team and that you will counsel them if they are not meeting their responsibilities. This should be presented simply in a straight forward, matter-of-a-fact manner. There should never be a situation where you will raise your voice or make fun of the team members.

One of the easiest ways to lose the respect of team members is to publicly criticize them. Publicly criticizing is a demeaning tactic that destroys any respect the leader might have had. Even the team members who are not being criticized will lose confidence in a leader who disrespects subordinates.

Foster trust and accountability

A strong leader shows the team members that he or she trusts them to do their job. The leader has to work in the middle ground between micromanaging everything and providing no oversight. You have to follow up to ensure that the job gets done. At the same time, the team members should be allowed the independence to do their job without constant interference.

Regular reporting sessions are often a productive way to share information and to maintain accountability. In these sessions, team members describe the progress they are making and what obstacles they have encountered. If problems have risen, the entire team can brainstorm solutions. This team communication process ensures that the team members know you trust them to carry out their responsibilities while, at the same time, emphasizing that they are accountable to you and also to the rest of the team.

Following through on the commitments that you make to the team is just as important as follow up on the team members responsibilities. If you shirk your responsibilities as the leader, team members will soon come to distrust you.

Pay attention to the details

An effective leader pays attention to the details. This is not to say that you have to be a micromanager. You want team members to feel that you trust them to do their jobs. However, at the same time, you need to make sure that the details of the job are not ignored.

I learned the importance of details when I was a restaurant manager. My regional supervisor at the time always checked the storeroom when he came into my restaurant. He wanted to make sure that all the labels on the canned goods in the store room were facing the same direction. I always made sure my employees kept the storeroom organized even though I wasn't totally convinced it was important. Later, when I became a regional supervisor, it became clear to me why he stressed this. The restaurants I visited that had managers who displayed the attention to the details such as the storeroom organization had cleaner facilities and provided better customer service than those where attention to detail was lacking. Details do matter.

Loyalty to the team and objectives

As a leader you cannot expect the team members to display a sense of loyalty to you and the team unless you display that same loyalty.

Similar to trust, loyalty goes both ways. When you display loyalty to the team and the team's objectives, the team members will reciprocate and show stronger loyalty to you. Don't expect any more consideration than you give.

The best way to demonstrate loyalty is to ensure that your team has the necessary resources to do their jobs. The resources can include everything from supplies and equipment to appropriate training. As the leader, it is your responsibility to help team members determine what resources are necessities and not luxuries that may be nice but are not actually crucial. Just because they ask for it doesn't mean it is actually essential.

However, when crucial resources are needed, you need to do everything you can to make sure the team has them. In some cases, this means taking the fight to upper management to make sure they understand why the particular resource is critical. The loyalty you show to the team members and their goals will go a long way to creating an atmosphere of trust, loyalty and accountability.

Acknowledge that you don't know it all

Confident leaders realize that they do not have all the answers. To be an effective leader, you do not need to be an expert in every aspect of your field. That is why you have the team. In the most effective teams, every team member brings in a unique set of knowledge, skills, and experience. Good leaders recognize that fact and capitalize on it.

I routinely watched leaders who refused to admit that they did not know something. They failed to listen to team members who had good ideas or who had relevant experience. This invariably led to an underperforming team. No one has all the answers. Effective leaders rely on the team members to offer suggestions and share ideas.

Key Reminders

- Take advice when appropriate, you don't have all the answers.
- Be truthful and generous, especially with praise.
- Display loyalty and the courage to stand up for what you believe is right.
- Hold team members and yourself accountable.
- Support your team and fight for resources.
- Be assertive rather than aggressive.
- Pay attention to the details.
- Walk the talk and follow through on your responsibilities.
- Ask for help when appropriate.
- Trust your team and make sure they can trust you.
- Listen.

CHAPTER 11 – SHARPEN YOUR LEADERSHIP SKILLS

The best leaders I have known all had one trait in common. They were always working to better themselves. They were introspective. They were regularly asking themselves, "What can I do to become a better leader?" Effective leadership takes practice, and the more we learn about what it takes to be a leader, the more effective we become as leaders.

Continue learning in your job

Knowledge inspires confidence, and confidence is important for leaders. If you as the leader display insecurity and hesitation, the team members will pick up on that. Learning all you can about your job is one of the most effective ways to gain confidence in your decisions. Study the details of the job. Take classes to increase your knowledge. Team up with others in your organization to share ideas and expertise.

When I was overseeing the faculty at a small private college, I was very knowledgeable about the roles and responsibilities of the faculty. I had started as a faculty member and eventually progressed into administration. I endeavored to sharpen my skills in two ways.

To be more informed about the role of the educator in a college setting I studied education theory through readings, seminars and conversations with experts. I also felt I needed to learn more about the other departments in the school. I sought out opportunities to work with the leaders of the admissions, financial aid, accounting, and human resources departments. I volunteered for cross-functional committees and met with the leaders of the other departments to learn about those departments. By continuing to discover as much as I could about the entire operation of the college, I was able to be more confident and effective as a leader of my department.

Study leadership

Good leaders also continue to learn all they can about leadership. Many organizations offer leadership classes for their employees. Sometimes these classes are part of a formal professional development process while, at other times they are presented as voluntary learning opportunities. Wise leaders take advantage of these opportunities. Even as an experienced leader, I attended countless workshops and seminars offered in the various organizations where I worked. I always learned something new when I attended on of these leadership education opportunities.

It is also an excellent idea to seek out opportunities outside of your workplace to learn more about leadership. Many local colleges and universities offer professional development courses. In most cases, these are open to members of the local community. These courses offer instruction in a variety of topics that are important to managers and leaders. They range from short half-day or day-long seminars to multi-week courses.

With a little online searching, you will find a wide variety of resources to learn more about leadership. You will find online blog posts, podcasts, videos, and courses that offer information about leadership. Much of it is free or very low-cost. You will also find several online educational companies that offer programs on leadership. There are endless ways to continue your leadership education.

Volunteer to gain experience

If you don't have very much practice in leading groups, I found that volunteering is a great way to build your leadership capability. Look for volunteer opportunities in your organization. I regularly offered to take on committee and task force assignments, and it was a valuable way to increase my experience as a leader. If possible, volunteer to lead the group. Leading a small group, even something as simple as a party planning committee, will give you valuable insights into the role of a leader and allow you to gain leadership skills.

Outside of the workplace, there is a limitless variety of community organizations, service organizations, and local committees that are always looking for additional members. Volunteering for these types of organizations will allow you to gain experience in a safe environment. Join the parents' organization at your child's school and then volunteer to lead a committee. Your contribution will be appreciated and the involvement with the group will be valuable for building leadership abilities.

Seek positive role models and find supportive allies

Are there individuals in your organization who impress you with their leadership skills? Get to know them. Observe how they interact with others. Learn what makes them effective in their positions. Use them as role models. Ideally, you will find a leader in your organization who will agree to serve as a mentor. These mentorship relationships are not only an excellent way to gain leadership expertise, but they will provide you greater visibility in the organization and enhance your reputation as a leader.

Look for role models outside your workplace. Study them. What characteristics make them particularly effective as leaders? Watch how they interact with other people. What qualities are most apparent? Seek out local leaders and ask for an interview. This informal research can give you clues into how you will want to conduct yourself when you are in a leadership role.

Read about great leaders. Over the years, I have learned a great deal about leadership by reading the biographies of respected leaders. From the U.S. presidents George Washington and Harry Truman to inspirational leaders such as Oprah Winfrey, Susan B. Anthony, Eleanor Roosevelt, Martin Luther King and Mahatma Gandhi, I read about what made them effective as leaders. I could take the behaviors and attitudes that they exhibited and apply them in my own leadership roles.

Ask for feedback

Good leaders are continually interested in knowing how they are doing. The best way to do that is to ask. Ask for advice from your supervisor. Your goal is twofold. You want to hear from them what they see you doing that is effective and you also want to learn about areas to improve.

Solicit feedback from your team. Their comments can give you clues to how they are reacting to your leadership style. When you are leading a team, conduct a regular check-in session where you ask what is going right and what is not going well. The insights gained from this type of dialogue will provide you with a good understanding about how well the team is working together, and it will often offer an indication of how you can improve your approach as a leader.

Practice humility

Exceptional leaders realize that they are only as effective as the teams they are leading. They are confident, yet they are not arrogant. They give credit where it is do and do not take all the credit themselves for the team's accomplishments. They have an open mind and realize that they have to continually strive to improve.

Good leaders admit that they don't have all the answers. They ask for help when it is needed. They recognize the experience and skills of the team members and encourage appropriate input from them. If you take away one thing from this book, the most valuable suggestion I can give is to ask yourself each day, "What can I do today to be a better leader?" And, every day take one action that will help you improve your leadership skills.

Key Reminders

- Learn all you can about leadership.
- Seek out classes and workshops about leadership.
- Read about the great leaders and ask yourself what made them successful.
- Gain leadership experience in volunteer organizations.
- Enlist a mentor for assistance.
- Listen to the feedback you receive and learn from it.

Made in the USA
San Bernardino, CA
29 June 2020